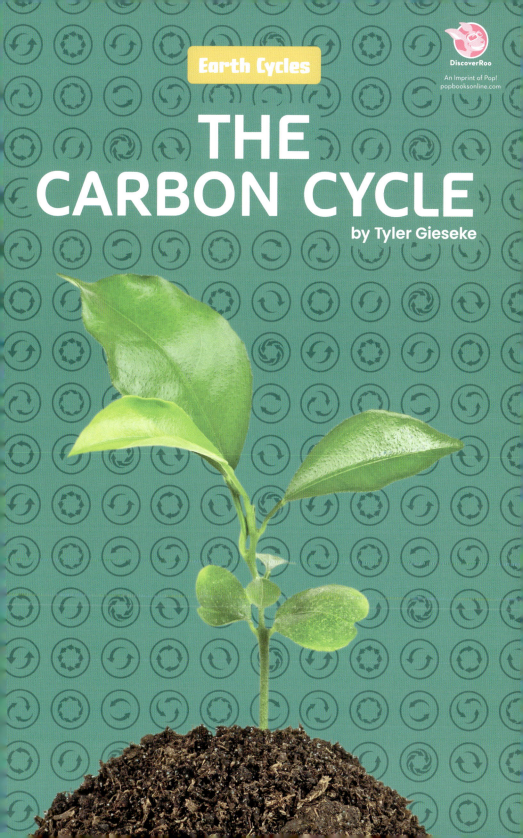

Earth Cycles

THE CARBON CYCLE

by Tyler Gieseke

DiscoverRoo
An Imprint of Pop!
popbooksonline.com

abdobooks.com

Published by Pop!, a division of ABDO, PO Box 398166, Minneapolis, Minnesota 55439. Copyright © 2023 by Abdo Consulting Group, Inc. International copyrights reserved in all countries. No part of this book may be reproduced in any form without written permission from the publisher. DiscoverRoo™ is a trademark and logo of Pop!.

Printed in the United States of America, North Mankato, Minnesota.

052022
092022

THIS BOOK CONTAINS RECYCLED MATERIALS

Cover Photo: Shutterstock Images
Interior Photos: Shutterstock Images
Editor: Elizabeth Andrews
Series Designer: Laura Graphenteen

Library of Congress Control Number: 2021951848
Publisher's Cataloging-in-Publication Data
Names: Gieseke, Tyler, author.
Title: The carbon cycle / by Tyler Gieseke.
Description: Minneapolis, Minnesota : Pop, 2023 | Series: Earth cycles | Includes online resources and index
Identifiers: ISBN 9781098242190 (lib. bdg.) | ISBN 9781098242893 (ebook)
Subjects: LCSH: Carbon cycle (Biogeochemistry)--Juvenile literature. | Atmospheric carbon dioxide--Juvenile literature. | Greenhouse gas mitigation--Juvenile literature. | Earth sciences--Juvenile literature. | Environmental sciences--Juvenile literature.
Classification: DDC 551.51--dc23

Pop open this book and you'll find QR codes loaded with information, so you can learn even more!

Scan this code* and others like it while you read, or visit the website below to make this book pop!

popbooksonline.com/carbon

*Scanning QR codes requires a web-enabled smart device with a QR code reader app and a camera.

TABLE OF CONTENTS

CHAPTER 1
The Stuff of Life 4

CHAPTER 2
Taking in Carbon 10

CHAPTER 3
Giving It Back 16

CHAPTER 4
Fossil Fuels 22

Making Connections. 30
Glossary 31
Index. 32
Online Resources 32

CHAPTER 1
THE STUFF OF LIFE

Carbon is a special material that helps build the bodies of plants and animals. All living things are made of carbon. Carbon starts out in the **environment**. Plants and animals take the carbon into

WATCH A VIDEO HERE!

Carbon is in people, plants, and animals.

their bodies. Later, it will travel back to the environment. This process is called the carbon cycle.

THE CARBON CYCLE

1: Plants take in carbon from the air during photosynthesis

2: **Herbivores** get carbon from plants

3: **Predators** get carbon from other animals

4: Breathing, plant and animal **decomposition**, and burning **fossil fuels** release carbon into the environment

Carbon is available in air and water. When plants grow, their bodies change the carbon into a form animals can use. Then, herbivores eat the plants. These animals use the plants' carbon in their own bodies. Finally, plants and animals release carbon back into the air. Dead **organisms** put carbon in the air and ground as they decompose.

DID YOU KNOW? Carbon that is stored in the ocean is called blue carbon.

The carbon cycle is an important Earth cycle. It provides the necessary material for life to grow on Earth. The carbon cycle also balances the amount of carbon stored in the environment and the amount stored inside organisms.

This balance can be fragile. Some carbon is stored in the ground as fossil fuels. When many humans burn these

 **DID YOU KNOW?** The places where large amounts of carbon are stored are called carbon sinks. Carbon sinks include the ocean, forests, and the air.

Burning fossil fuels creates energy.

fuels in cars and factories, a lot of carbon goes into the air all at once. This leads to many problems, including climate change. Understanding the carbon cycle is important!

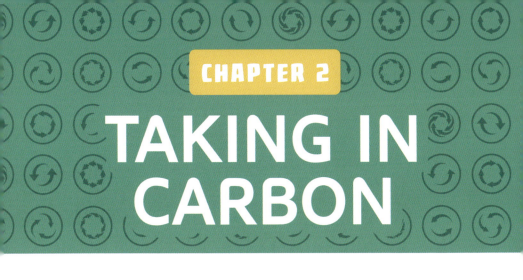

CHAPTER 2
TAKING IN CARBON

Carbon dioxide (CO_2) is a gas in air and water. It has carbon in it. But plants and animals can't use the carbon in that form. Plants pull the carbon out of the CO_2!

LEARN MORE HERE!

When water is choppy, it mixes with air.

Plants take in CO_2 from the air and water. During photosynthesis, plants make their own food using water, CO_2, and sunlight. The plants' bodies transform the water and CO_2 into sugars and oxygen. The sugars contain carbon and help the plants build up their bodies. Then the plants release the oxygen into the air around them. Photosynthesis is the first step in the carbon cycle.

DID YOU KNOW? Carbon is used in DNA, the substance in every cell that tells the body how to grow and change.

Animals take in carbon when they eat fruit.

In the second step, **herbivores** eat the plants. The animals' bodies use the carbon in the plants to make them stronger. Herbivores are animals that get all the carbon they need from plants. They do not eat other animals. Rabbits, deer, and many types of birds are herbivores.

Tigers are predators and at the top of their food web.

Some animals eat don't eat plants or don't eat them very often. Instead, these animals mostly eat other animals.

These animals are called **predators**. Predators do not get their carbon from plants. Instead, they use the carbon in herbivores' bodies to build up their own bodies. This is the third step of the carbon cycle.

FOOD WEBS

Carbon moves from plants to herbivores and predators in patterns called food webs. Food webs map out eating relationships in an **ecosystem**. For example, the plants of a forest ecosystem include bushes and grass. They are at the bottom of the food web. Deer eat bushes but not grass, while rabbits eat both. These animals are above the plants in the food web. Raccoons would be a level higher. They eat rabbits but not deer. Cougars would be even higher in the web.

CHAPTER 3
GIVING IT BACK

Plants and animals return carbon to the air in the form of CO_2. This is the fourth step of the carbon cycle. Animals release CO_2 into the **environment** when they breathe out.

EXPLORE LINKS HERE!

Animals take in oxygen and send out CO_2 when they breathe.

Plants and animals also give back their carbon by dying. **Decomposers** break down the bodies of dead plants and animals and eat some of the nutrients. These **organisms** include bacteria, earthworms, and fungi. When the decomposers do their work, they put CO_2 into the air.

Some of the carbon from dead plants and animals can end up in the earth. Over a very long time, the carbon in the earth can become

Mushrooms and other fungi are decomposers.

buried deep beneath the surface. Then, volcanoes release it into the air as CO_2 gas when they erupt! This is another step in the carbon cycle.

Oil is a fossil fuel that is pumped out of the ground.

There is even another way that carbon returns to the air. Some living things that decomposed a very long time ago turn into **fossil fuels**. Fossil fuels include natural gas and **coal**. They are buried deep in the earth. Humans dig them up to use in cars and factories.

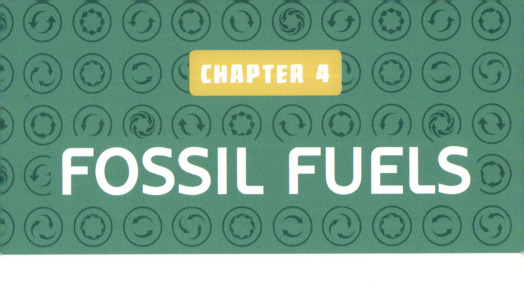

CHAPTER 4
FOSSIL FUELS

The carbon cycle usually keeps a good balance between the amount of carbon in the air and the amount of carbon in animals, plants, and the ground. It is a natural system.

Human beings have burned large amounts of **fossil fuels** over the past 300

COMPLETE AN ACTIVITY HERE!

Logging provides wood and makes way for buildings.

years. This put much more CO_2 into the air than plants can take in. Also, people have cut down lots of trees to make paper products. So, there are fewer plants to take CO_2 out of the air.

Wildfires release lots of smoke into the air.

Too much carbon dioxide in the air causes problems. CO_2 traps heat from the Sun and keeps the Earth warm. This is a good thing! But with too much CO_2 in the air, the average temperature on Earth is rising quickly.

A warmer Earth brings climate change. Ice in the **Arctic** is melting. This makes the sea rise and flood some islands and coasts. Weather events are also changing. Scientists say there will be more extreme storms and wildfires over time. These can destroy buildings and hurt people!

DID YOU KNOW? The amount of CO_2 in the air is going up by about four percent every ten years.

Understanding the carbon cycle is important. It helps scientists see how climate change is happening. And, it helps them find ways to slow it down.

Nature's beauty is possible because of carbon.

Carbon is the stuff of life. But the carbon cycle is just one of the many incredible Earth cycles.

Step 1: Plants take carbon dioxide (CO_2) out of the air during photosynthesis

Step 2: Herbivores eat plants

Step 3: Predators eat herbivores

Step 4: Breathing, **decomposition**, and **fossil fuels** release CO_2 into the air

Cycle begins again

CO_2

human breathing

dead organisms and waste products

fossil fuels

MAKING CONNECTIONS

TEXT-TO-SELF

Did you know anything about the carbon cycle before reading this book? What did you learn that was new?

TEXT-TO-TEXT

Have you read other books about Earth cycles? How are those cycles similar to and different from the carbon cycle?

TEXT-TO-WORLD

What parts of your daily routine use fossil fuels?

GLOSSARY

Arctic — the cold, northern section of Earth.

coal — a black, solid carbon-based fuel.

decompose — to break down after death. Decomposers are organisms that break down dead plants and animals.

ecosystem — the interactions between living things in a particular place.

environment — the surrounding area.

fossil fuels — buried energy sources made of long-dead organisms.

herbivore — an animal that eats only plants.

organism — a living thing.

predator — an animal that hunts other animals for food.

INDEX

carbon dioxide (CO_2), 10, 12, 16, 18–19, 23–25, 28–29

climate change, 9, 25–26

decomposing, 6, 7, 18, 21, 28–29

fossil fuels, 6, 8–9, 21–22, 29

herbivores, 6–7, 13, 15, 28–29

photosynthesis, 6, 12, 28–29

predators, 6, 15, 29

ONLINE RESOURCES
popbooksonline.com

Scan this code* and others like it while you read, or visit the website below to make this book pop!

popbooksonline.com/carbon

*Scanning QR codes requires a web-enabled smart device with a QR code reader app and a camera.